Automating Personal Finance

Smart Tools for Wealth-Management

Table of Contents

Chapter 1. Introduction

In the ever-evolving world of personal finance, a revolution is quietly taking place, powered by the fusion of technology and wealth management: it's the era of automating personal finances. Our Special Report "Automating Personal Finance: Smart Tools for Wealth Management" proposes to navigate you through this modern, money-wise landscape. Don't worry if you're not technically inclined! Our report takes an easy-to-understand approach, demystifying complex theories, unravelling the digital lexicon and introducing the magic of automation in plain, everyday language. This report holds the potential to empower you, equipping you with smart tools and strategies to automate your finances and build wealth like a pro. Dive in, and experience how a few clicks can redefine your financial outlook and pave the way for an abundant future. Welcome to the new era of wealth-management, and yes, it's all within your reach.

Chapter 2. The New Face of Personal Finance: Automation

The times are changing, and so is the face of managing your personal finances. Automation—this is the word that describes the transformation happening in the world of personal finance. The old method of manual bookkeeping with its clutter of paper receipts, transaction slips, and laborious account reconciliation tasks is crumbling away under the onslaught of digitized financial management techniques.

Automation, at its heart, is meant to simplify complicated tasks or sequences of work. Similar principles, when applied to personal finance, can streamline your financial tasks, optimize your time, and ultimately, lead to more wealth.

2.1. The Wheel of Automation

It's important to understand the cycle of automation which consists of the following steps: Gather, Analyze, Plan, Act, and Review.

1. **Gather**: This is the step where you bring together all your financial information. Think of it as collecting puzzle pieces and storing them in one place. Important data points include income (from all sources), expenses, assets, liabilities, and investment details.

2. **Analyze**: In this step, the data collected is processed to locate patterns or trends. This analysis can be crucial in revealing the health of your financial situation.

3. **Plan**: Based on the analysis, you create a customized personal finance plan. This includes creating a budget, outlining an

investment strategy, setting financial goals, and noting the steps needed to achieve these goals.

4. **Act**: After planning, it is time to execute your plan. This might involve changes in spending habits, starting new investments, or repaying pending debts.

5. **Review**: At regular intervals, your financial situation and plan must be re-evaluated, and necessary adjustments must be made.

The power of automation is in streamlining these steps, allowing you to have a transparent view of your financial health and to make educated money decisions.

2.2. Automation Tools Revolutionize Personal Finance

Technology has been a game-changer in the realm of personal finance, giving birth to a slew of tools and applications that help individuals not just manage their money but also grow it. Here are few noteworthy ones:

1. **Budgeting Tools**: Apps like Mint and PocketGuard pull data from your bank accounts and credit cards to help you create and manage your budget. They also provide timely alerts to keep you in check.

2. **Investment Management Tools**: These include apps like Betterment and Robinhood which automate your investments, aligning them with your financial goals and appetite for risk. They perform regular portfolio realignments and tax-loss harvesting to optimize returns.

3. **Bill Payment and Debt Management Tools**: These digital tools ensure you never miss bill payments and help you keep a check on unnecessary interest charges. They can also help you strategize repayment to effectively manage your liabilities.

4. **Retirement and Financial Goal Planning Tools**: Platforms like Personal Capital help you track your long-term financial goals like retirement, children's education fund, etc. They provide detailed insight into your progress and help you plan effectively.

5. **Expense Tracking Tools**: They record and categorize each one of your expenses, providing a clear picture of where your money goes. This helps in identifying trends and areas of potential saving.

2.3. Embracing Automation: A Step-by-Step Guide

If automation is such a boon, you must be wondering how to transition into it. Here's a step-by-step guide for a smooth transition into automating your personal finances:

1. **Understand Your Financial Situation**: The first part is to fully understand your current financial standing. This includes realizing your income sources, expenses, existing debts, and financial goals.

2. **Choosing the Right Tools**: Not every financial tool might be suitable for you as they cater to different individual needs. Choose tools that are intuitive, user-friendly and meet your unique requirements.

3. **Setting Up Automation**: After setting up your accounts with the chosen tools, it is time to input the necessary information and preferences. Be meticulous during this step to ensure the platform understands you and your financial needs.

4. **Monitor and Control**: While automation does take some day-to-day tasks off your plate, it doesn't mean you should trust the bots blindly. Regular monitoring and intervention are critical to ensure everything is on the right track.

5. **Evaluating Success**: It's important to periodically evaluate the

success of automated tools to ensure they're helping to meet your financial goals. If necessary, adjustments can be made or even switch to better-suited apps.

The advent of automation in personal finance promises a world of financial management that's more unified, clearer, less time-consuming, and above all, more efficient. It's time to embrace this new era, repurpose technology to your advantage, and set foot on the path of financial freedom. The new face of personal finance—automation—is truly the dawn of an era that promises simplicity and smart wealth management.

Chapter 3. Understanding Financial Automation Tools

The sophistication and ubiquity of technology in financial management has introduced a new era of automated personal finance. In this exciting landscape, an array of digital tools are ready to elevate your personal wealth management game. Whether you want to budget more effectively, digitalize investment strategies, or automate retirement savings, there exists an application to cater to your needs. In an uncomplicated, plain language manner, let's delve into these financial automation tools for a comprehensive understanding.

3.1. The Basics: What are Financial Automation Tools?

Financial automation tools refer to technology-aided platforms and digital services designed to manage, track, and enhance your personal finances. These tools aptly blend financial knowledge with advanced technology to aid in budgeting, investing, saving, and even tax planning. The rising adoption of these tools marks a shift in personal finance manangement from manual paper-ledgers and human advisors to digitally managed portfolios and automated investment schemes, simplifying financial management at an individual level.

3.2. Categorizing Financial Automation Tools

While all financial automation tools share the ultimate goal of assisting with personal finance management, they can be divided into several broad categories based on functionality:

1. Budgeting Tools: Applications such as Mint and You Need A Budget (YNAB) help users track their expenditure, delineate budgets, and strategize spending.

2. Investment Tools: Robo-advisors like Betterment and Wealthfront make investing easier by automatically creating and managing diversified portfolios.

3. Savings Tools: Platforms like Qapital and Digit automate savings by rounding up purchases to the nearest dollar and then investing the difference.

4. Debt Reduction Tools: Services like Tally and Trim assist in managing and reducing debts.

These categories aren't exhaustive or mutually exclusive. Many tools cross categories and provide a suite of functions.

3.3. Characteristics of Effective Financial Automation Tools

As diverse and plentiful these digital tools are, picking the right one requires understanding of their purpose. Let's examine some of the defining features to consider while selecting a financial automation tool:

1. User-friendly Interface: An intuitive interface ensures that users, regardless of their digital familiarity, can navigate the service effectively.

2. Customization: An effective tool allows for personalization to match the user's financial goal and risk appetite.

3. Security: Given the amount of confidential financial data involved, stringent security measures are non-negotiable.

4. Customer Support: Prompt and effective customer support is vital, especially when dealing with complex financial decisions.

5. Transparent Fees: Service must clearly state its fee structure upfront to avoid hidden costs.

6. Integration: The tool should be capable of syncing with multiple financial accounts for comprehensive management.

3.4. The Impact of Automation on Personal Finance

As financial automation tools bring financial advisors' expertise and sophisticated strategies to everyone's reach, they are democratizing wealth building. Here's a closer look at the impact:

1. Time-saving: By automating, people can avoid time-consuming and burdensome everyday financial tasks such as bill payments, budgeting, and investments.

2. Eliminating Human Errors: Automation helps in reducing errors resulting from manual data entry and calculation.

3. Enhancing Financial Literacy: These tools guide users through complex financial concepts, promoting overall financial literacy.

4. Democratizing Investment Strategy: Traditional wealth-management services usually require substantial investments. But many financial automation tools have low or no minimum investment threshold, making wealth management accessible.

3.5. How to Implement Automation in Your Personal Finance

Embracing automation in personal finance involves a few key steps:

1. Identify Your Financial Goals: Understand what you aim to achieve is the first step. Goals can range from savings for retirement, investing for wealth accumulation, or managing a

budget.

2. Select Suitable Tools: Depending on your goals, select tools that are designed to support those objectives.

3. Customize Your Plan: Most tools have customizable features. Tailor these according to your preferences and goals.

4. Monitor Regularly: Even after automation, it's crucial to monitor these tools to ensure they are functioning towards achieving your objectives.

The world of automated finances can seem complex, but with the array of user-friendly tools now available, integrating technology into your personal financial management is easier than ever. As we move into this exciting new era of automation, we invite you to explore the wealth of options at your disposal to simplify your finance management and turn your dreams of financial security into reality.

Chapter 4. Keys to Effective Budgeting with Automation

Understanding your income and expenses while planning for future needs is the cornerstone of financial health. Budgeting, seen by many as a tedious and time-consuming task, transforms into an effortless exercise when automation steps in. By harnessing the power of modern technology, you can design, implement, monitor, and improve your financial plan at the click of a button.

===The Foundation: Understanding Your Current Financial Situation.

Before creating an automated budget, it's crucial to grasp where your finances stand today. This requires a clear understanding of all avenues of income, current monthly responsibilities, one-off expenses, savings and investments.

To facilitate this, first jot down your total net income from all sources. This figure will be the cornerstone of your budget and include your salary, bonuses, rental income, dividends and any other.

Next, capture all your expenses, whether necessary or discretionary. Necessary expenses can be mortgage or rent, utilities, debt repayments and groceries. Discretionary expenses can include entertainment, dining out, vacations and shopping. Be distinct and precise: these numbers will form the architecture of your spending plan.

Don't forget to record your savings and investments. This will provide a comprehensive view of your financial profile and help you allocate funds to meet future needs.

===The Blueprint: Formulating a Budget Plan

Using the above data, outline a financial plan. A common and effective model is the 50/30/20 rule. According to this rule, allocate 50% of your income towards essential expenses, 30% towards discretionary items, and 20% towards savings and investment.

You may need to tweak this according to your profile and goals - the key is to devise a system that works for you. Once this plan gets a final shape, it's time to automate.

===The Tools: Leveraging Technology

There's a wide array of financial tools available that make this process simpler and more efficient. Some popular tools are Mint, YNAB (You Need A Budget), and Quicken. These tools can link to your bank accounts, credit cards, loans, and investments, giving you a real-time overview of your financial world.

They also categorize and track your expenses, alerting you when you're about to exceed your set limit. Moreover, these tools allow you to set financial goals and track your progress towards them with minimal intervention on your part.

===The Implementation: Automating Your Financial Plan

Once you have your plan and tool in place, the next step is to automate as much as possible. Ideally, you want to set up automatic transfers to cover your bills, savings, and investments immediately when your paycheck hits your account.

Most banks offer this facility, ensuring your money gets distributed before you have the chance to spend it. This eliminates the risk of missed payments, late fees and takes the stress out of managing manual transfers.

For expenses that can't be automated, such as one-off expenses or cash spending, leverage the tools to set alerts. These reminders can prevent overspending and keep you within the boundaries of your budget.

===The Benefits: Advantages of Automating Your Financial Plan

Beyond the convenience and time saved, the automation of your budgeting process offers you improved control over your finances. It can lead to better saving habits, more directed investments, less debt, and a more robust emergency fund. Moreover, it leaves little room for human error, ensuring your financial plan moves smoothly month on month.

===The Pitfalls: Potential Challenges in Automating Budgeting

Although automating your budgeting process brings several advantages, it's not without challenges. Be aware that automated payments can lead to 'set and forget' scenarios where you might not monitor your finances as closely as you should. To avoid this, schedule periodic reviews of your financial plan and make adjustments as necessary.

Also, while financial tools offer convenience, they usually link directly to your financial accounts, which could raise privacy and security concerns. Always ensure the tools you choose employ robust security measures to protect your personal information.

===The Future: A Forward-Looking Financial Plan

As you progress in your career and personal life, your budget will require adjustments to cater to changing incomes, expenses, and goals. The flexibility that comes with automating your budget allows for easy modifications as these changes occur.

Don't forget to check in frequently and make necessary updates to remain aligned with your financial vision. With a solid automated budget, you're not just planning for the current phase, but for a financially secure future and an abundant retirement.

The new era of wealth management is here, and it's automated. Embrace the magical fusion of finances and technology. With a few clicks, you enter the driver's seat of your financial journey. Empowered, equipped, and ready to build an affluent future. No more manual hassle, no more forgetting due dates - just a smart, precise, and efficient road to wealth creation.

Chapter 5. Potent Savings Tools: Revolutionising Money Management

Just as automation has shaped many other aspects of our lives, the world of personal finance has experienced its own digital evolution. This chapter will delve into the digital tools currently on the market that allow anyone, regardless of financial expertise, to automate their savings and investment strategies. These instruments can potentially revolutionise how we manage our money and are consequently propelling us into a new era of financial abundance.

5.1. Power of Automated Savings

Before we discuss specific tools, it is important to understand the underlying philosophy that makes automated savings so potent. Automated savings is essentially a regular, automatic transfer from your checking account into a savings or investment account. The key idea here is "out of sight, out of mind." You are less likely to miss money that you never had a chance to spend. Plus, with the effect of compound interest, these regular, small amounts can add up to substantial savings over time.

To give you a sense of the power of automation, consider this example: let's suppose you set up an automatic transfer of $200 every month into a savings account or investment fund that yields an average of 5% interest annually. In 30 years, you'll have amassed over $200,000 from your transfers alone – plus over $150,000 in interest!

5.2. Tools for Automatic Savings

Now let's explore some tools that can help you achieve this automated savings strategy. Many online banking systems offer the ability to set up automatic transfers. However, there are several fintech tools, apps, and platforms that take this concept to the next level.

One of them is Digit. Digit tracks your spending habits and identifies safe opportunities to transfer money from your checking account into savings. Another is Acorns, which round up your purchases to the nearest dollar and invests the spare change in a diversified portfolio. Chime, another popular financial app, offers an automatic savings feature that rounds up transactions and transfers the difference to savings.

Although their methodologies vary, all these tools work on the same principle: they find opportunities within your ordinary spending habits to build your savings automatically, helping you to save consistently without drastically affecting your lifestyle.

5.3. Tools for Automated Investments

While savings are an essential part of a robust financial plan, wise investing is what truly grows wealth. Fortunately, the fintech industry has done a commendable job in democratising investment options, making it easier for anyone to start investing without needing a significant amount of starting capital or intricate financial knowledge.

Betterment, a pioneer in robo-advisors, offers personalised investment portfolios based on your goals and risk tolerance. Once your preferences are set, Betterment automates your investment management, including allocating funds and rebalancing your portfolio when necessary.

Apps like Stash also make investing easier by teaching you how to start investing with as little as $5. Stash offers fractional shares, allowing users to buy portions of stocks and ETFs. You can automate your investments at scheduled intervals to seamlessly grow your portfolio over time.

Wealthfront, another popular robo-advisor, provides automated investment management and financial planning tools. It helps users create diversified portfolios and optimise their investments for tax efficiency, while maintaining the desired level of risk.

These are just a few examples of the automated investment tools available. Remember that, while all of them can do the groundwork for you, it will still be of immense value to understand the basics of investing and stay informed about your portfolio's performance.

5.4. Overcoming Hurdles with Automation

Despite the potential benefits of automated savings and investment tools, it's important to confront the potential concerns that users may have. The first concern involves trust: Can automatic platforms be relied on completely? While it's true that these tools have benefited from advancements in machine learning and algorithms, there can be little replacement for human involvement and oversight. It's crucial to review your accounts regularly and stay familiar with your financial standing.

Privacy and security concerns also stand among potential hurdles. Rest assured, most fintech companies are aware of the importance of protecting personal information and adhere to strict data security standards to keep your information secure. However, always remember to keep your devices secure, use strong, unique passwords, and be careful about sharing any sensitive information.

5.5. Transforming Your Financial Future

As we wrap up this exploration of automated savings and investment tools, remember that the purpose of these tools is to make wealth creation more accessible. They are designed to help you achieve consistent savings, operational efficiency, and steady wealth accumulation, all while requiring minimal effort on your part.

Despite its potential, automated finance could never entirely replace human intentionality and initiative in financial matters. It can, however, act as a powerful ally to those with the wisdom to wield it well. So go ahead, and take the first steps towards automating your finances, simplifying your wealth management process, and revolutionising your financial future.

Ultimately, the era of automated personal finance is about much more than monetary benefits or convenience – it's about empowering individuals to take control of their financial destiny with confidence, effectiveness, and peace of mind. It's time to enter into a new phase of financial evolution and make the most of these potent savings and investment tools.

Chapter 6. Investing Simplified Through Automated Platforms

In the current personal finance landscape, a rapidly growing subset of wealth management tools allows individuals, from beginners to seasoned investors, an opportunity to dip their feet in the investment realm-- they're known as Automated Investment Platforms (AIPs). Also known as robo-advisors, these platforms have democratized investing by automating complex tasks, allowing users to establish and grow their investment portfolios without needing exhaustive knowledge of financial markets, facilitating a simplified investment experience. Let us explore them in significant detail.

6.1. Understanding Automated Investment Platforms

Automated Investment Platforms use advanced algorithms and financial models to automate the process of investing. Powered by cutting-edge technology, these platforms ask users a series of questions to assess their financial situation and goals, then construct a highly tailored portfolio designed to maximize return for a given level of risk, adjusted to the investor's comfort levels.

AIPs provide a low-cost and convenient alternative to traditional, resource intensive investment methods. They are always online, so you can access them anywhere, anytime. The platforms provide users with ongoing portfolio management, including automatic asset rebalancing and tax-loss harvesting, eliminating the hassles of manual account management.

6.2. The Benefits of Using Automated Investment Platforms

AIPs come with a host of advantages. They are, notably:

- Accessibility: They open the world of investable assets to everyone, not just to the financially savvy or wealthier individuals.

- Affordability: Compared to traditional investing, robo-advisors often demand lower initial investment amounts and charge smaller fees.

- Simplicity: They streamline the investing process by automating it, taking complex financial concepts and presenting them in simple, understandable ways.

- Efficiency: As AIPs provide automatic rebalancing, they ensure that your portfolio maintains its target asset allocation, saving you from emotionally-driven investment decisions.

6.3. The Process of Solving Your Investing Needs

Automated Investment Platforms facilitate a typically three-step process.

1. Establish Your Goals - You begin by answering a questionnaire designed to evaluate your financial status, risk tolerance, and investment objectives. This step helps create a personal investor profile for you, which is crucial in defining your investment strategy.

2. Create a Unique Portfolio - Based on your investor profile, the platforms generate a tailored portfolio. This portfolio typically consists of a diversified blend of assets, usually low-cost ETFs or

Index Funds, aimed at achieving your investment goals while fitting into your risk comfort zone.

3. Ongoing Management - Once your portfolio is set up, the platform takes care of the ongoing management. This includes automatic rebalancing to keep your investments on track with your goals and periodic reevaluation of your strategy to ensure it remains the most effective based on your changing needs and market conditions.

6.4. Risks and Limitations

While AIPs simplify investing, they have limitations and come with their risks, which all investors should keep in mind. A chief limitation is that if you want to invest in individual stocks or bonds, most AIPs may not offer the option. Furthermore, despite AIPs providing automated tax-loss harvesting, they cannot replace the personalized advice a tax professional can provide.

AIPs use algorithms to build portfolios based on historical data, which assumes that future market behavior will mirror the past. However, markets can be unpredictable, and the algorithm may fall short during sudden changes in market conditions.

Despite this, Automated Investment Platforms are remarkably effective at automating and simplifying investing. They're not a complete solution, but they're a fantastic tool to help anyone, regardless of financial acumen, begin their journey into financial wealth building.

6.5. Closing Thoughts: Embrace the Automation

Automated Investment Platforms have significantly leveled the investing playing field, providing access to sound investing strategies that were once only available to individuals with substantial wealth or financial knowledge. By integrating user-friendly interfaces and sophisticated investment algorithms, these platforms facilitate a simplified and accessible investment experience.

It's time to embrace the future. However, as with any financial decision, it behooves the user to research thoroughly, understanding both the potential benefits and risks, before confidently embarking on this journey.

Chapter 7. Retirement Planning: Automated Solutions

The essence of retirement planning is ensuring you have enough resources to live on after retirement. Previously, retirement planning was a tedious task involving manual calculations, numerous spreadsheets, and an understanding of complex financial jargon. However, automation is now redefining this process, promising an easier, accurate, and streamlined retirement planning journey.

7.1. Automating Sources of Income

The first step towards retirement planning lies in understanding and automating your sources of income. This isn't merely about having regular cash flows, but ensuring they're optimized for your retirement goals. Automation tools provide a holistic view of your income sources, whether they are pensions, investments, annuities, or social security benefits.

Baseline function includes consolidating your income information in one place and providing forecasts based on variables such as inflation rate, investment returns, and policy changes. The sophistication level of some tools enables scenario planning. For instance, you can simulate what happens if you delay starting the withdrawal of social security benefits. This enables hands-on control of your retirement income, while eliminating the need for manual calculations.

7.2. Streamlining Expenses Monitoring

Retirement planning goes beyond income; managing and forecasting expenses is a significant aspect, too. Knowing where your money goes each month is a cornerstone for setting realistic retirement goals. Automated solutions offer the ease of tracking expenses, categorizing them, and analyzing future spending patterns.

Such platforms can synchronize with your bank accounts and credit cards, analyzing spending patterns seamlessly. Simultaneously, they allow for manual input of expenses that may not be channelized through your bank, such as cash transactions and others. With a complete picture of your spending habits, these automated tools can predict future expenses based on past trends, life expectancy, and healthcare needs.

7.3. Navigating the Investment Landscape

Investment is a critical component of retirement planning, and its automation makes it both efficient and manageable, especially for non-experts. Robo-advisers, the vanguard of automated investing, use algorithms to allocate, construct, manage and optimize an investment portfolio based on a client's desired level of risk and targeted retirement date.

These platforms tend to offer lower fees than human advisers, making them an ideal option to build wealth for retirement. Automated rebalancing is another feature, ensuring adherence to asset allocation goals over time. Robo-advisers can steer clear of emotion-led investing mistakes, and often propose diversified portfolios that can weather market variances and inflation.

7.4. Tax Optimizations Strategies

Automated retirement planning tools can also guide you through tax implications associated with retirement. Retirement accounts are taxed differently and planning for these required deductions can prevent unpleasant surprises in the future.

The tax-optimization feature in these tools help minimize the tax bill. They consider factors like tax-brackets, capital gain tax, and the tax-efficiency of different account types. Additionally, these tools can automate withdrawals from retirement accounts in the most tax-efficient manner.

7.5. Health Care Cost Projections

Health-related expenses are often the most unpredictable variables in retirement planning. With increasing age, the chances increases for more regular and significant healthcare expenses. An effective retirement planning tool will automate the process of estimating potential healthcare costs, including long-term care.

Through robust modeling techniques, these tools consider many factors like current health status, family medical history, and general trends in healthcare cost inflation. Consequently, you are better prepared for this significant aspect of retirement expense without having to dive deep into health economics.

7.6. Estate Planning Simplified

Thinking about the distribution of assets might be uncomfortable but is an essential part of retirement planning. Automation in this area simplifies the process of will creation, assigning executors, and designating power of attorney. An automated estate planning tool typically comes with prompts that reduce the possibility of errors and omissions.

A sophisticated tool will go beyond the basics and delve into the implications of laws in different states, tax implications, and even options for charitable donations. Leverage automation to ensure a straightforward transition of your assets, minimizing the potential for family strife and litigation.

While automation simplifies personal finance, it is no replacement for human intuition and imagination. Therefore, regularly reviewing and ensuring that your automated plans fits into your larger life strategy becomes vital. As the age-old saying goes, "Keep your tools sharp." Stay on top of advancements in automation technologies in this critical life aspect for the smart and worry-free management of retirement plans. Welcome this new era of automated retirement planning to stay financially prosperous even in your golden days.

Chapter 8. User-Friendly Apps Promoting Debt Management

In an increasingly digital world, managing your money effectively is a lot easier when you can leverage the flexibility and convenience of user-friendly apps. These tools are designed to make everything, from tracking your expenses to managing your debts, as simple as a few taps on your phone. Robust, intuitive and data-driven, these apps are a godsend, especially for individuals working to reduce or eliminate their debt.

8.1. Understanding Debt Management Apps

Debt management apps are digital platforms designed to provide handy and convenient solutions for tracking and managing your debts. Different apps have different specific features and strengths, but all have the overarching goal of helping users understand, reduce, and eventually eliminate their debts. They allow users to visualize their debt in a manner that is more tangible, and thereby take a controlled and managed approach to repay it.

Many debt management apps employ strategies like the snowball or avalanche methods to debt repayment, allowing users to gradually chip away at their debts by focusing either on eliminating small debts first, or those with the highest interest rates.

8.2. Features of Debt Management Apps

While there is a range of financial management apps available, a good debt management app will include pivotal features that aid in debt reduction and overall financial wellness. Some of the key features you can anticipate include:

1. Synchronization with financial accounts: This allows users to link all their financial sources, including bank accounts and credit cards, making it easy to track and manage everything in one place.

2. Customized debt repayment plan: Based on a user's financial situation and preferences, the app crafts a plan to help them tackle their debts.

3. Regular reminders and notifications: Regular notifications about payments, upcoming dues, or potential savings keep users on track.

4. Goal setting and progress tracking: Users can set their financial goals, and the app tracks their performance, creating reports that indicate their progress.

5. Financial education: Many of these apps offer educative resources to help users understand debt management and other personal finance aspects.

8.3. Evaluating Debt Management Apps

When it comes to choosing a debt management app, it's important to consider several factors:

1. User Interface: A clean, user-friendly interface helps individuals

to understand their financial data and navigate their way around the app.

2. Security: Since these apps involve syncing bank details, confirmation of the security of your data is paramount.

3. Affordability: Some apps charge a monthly or annual fee for premium features. Make sure to pick an app that delivers value for its cost.

4. Customization: Look for an app that allows you to personalize your financial strategies, payment reminders, and more.

5. Customer support: It's wise to opt for an app with robust customer support in case complications arise.

8.4. Popular Debt Management Apps

There are numerous debt management apps in the market, each with a unique proposition designed to help users manage and eliminate their debts. Here's a list of a few popular ones to check out:

1. **Mint**: Mint is a free-to-use versatile app that provides a clear overview of your financial picture. It allows easy budgeting, goal setting, credit monitoring, and tracking of all your accounts in one place.

2. **YNAB (You Need A Budget)**: YNAB's primary focus is on budgeting and living within your means. It helps users allocate every dollar they earn towards specific 'jobs' like expenses, savings, or debt repayment.

3. **Undebt.it**: Undebt.it is excellent for those learning about different debt repayment strategies. It offers multiple repayment plan options, including snowball and avalanche methods.

4. **Debt Payoff Planner and Tracker**: This app helps users create a debt repayment plan. It provides detailed charts and progress reports.

5. **PocketGuard**: PocketGuard offers insight into spending habits, allowing users to manage their money better. It helps users stay on top of their bills, expenditure, and savings, making it a handy tool for those working to reduce debt.

Technology has made debt management simple and effective while on the go. By using these debt management apps, you can efficiently manage your finances and debt, making a positive stride towards an abundant financial future. Remember, the journey to financial success often begins with the right tool in hand. So, choose wisely and let your financial stress be a thing of the past.

Chapter 9. Unlocking Financial Freedom Through Automation

Entering the realm of financial freedom can seem like a daunting task. However, by leveraging the transformative power of automation, it becomes not only possible, but achievable over a realistic timeframe. We are in the age of technological marvels where the very definition of money management is changing. Here's how you can harness that change.

9.1. Understanding Financial Automation

Financial automation, in its most basic form, refers to the tactic of using technology to handle financial tasks. By leveraging high-tech tools and digital services, you can streamline your financial management, achieving optimal results with minimal effort. This includes tasks such as bill payments, investments, savings, budgeting, alerts, tracking spending, and more.

Automatic bill payments can help individuals avoid late fees, uphold good credit scores, and reduce stress regarding deadlines. Investments can be set to be regular and increase in step with raises, ensuring that as income grows, so too does the investment portfolio. Auto transfers to a savings account ensures that you pay yourself first, and money set aside is not accidentally spent. By looking at the past patterns of your spending, you can also set bounds on various spending categories, and allow your automation system to warn you when you are nearing, or have crossed your budget.

However, financial automation is not without its pitfalls. The ease of "setting and forgetting" may lead to costs going unnoticed. Always remember the importance of keeping an eye on your finances, even as you use tools to help manage them. Also, if you live paycheck-to-paycheck, automated savings may end up causing overdrafts or missed necessary payments, a problem that would have been apparent with manual management.

Therefore, financial automation should be integrated into a broader strategy of financial wellbeing, being only one part of a multi-pronged approach.

9.2. Unveiling the Tools of Financial Automation

There's a wide array of tools, both free and paid, to aid your financial automation journey. Ranging from Bill Pay services through your bank, to investment applications like E*Trade or Robinhood, to comprehensive personal finance management systems like Quicken, Mint and Personal Capital.

These tools offer different benefits, but generally are designed to make it easier to keep track of and manage your finances from one place. They can auto-categorize your spending, help design budgets, set goals for saving, and even manage your investments.

Choosing the tools that are best suited to you can depend on a number of factors. Your comfort level with technology, specific requirements, lifestyle, and comfort level with having your financial information stored by a third party all come into play. Exploring the different options available, and testing tools can help determine what works best for you.

9.3. Hop on the Investment Automaton

Investment is one area where automation can provide significant benefits. Robo-advisors are algorithm-based platforms that manage investment portfolios, reducing the need for a traditional investment advisor. They provide financial advice or investment management online with some level of human intervention.

Notable platforms include Betterment, Wealthfront, and Vanguard, which can automate everything from the allocation of investments to tax-loss harvesting. The key benefit is that it can offer sophisticated investment techniques, such as re-balancing and tax optimization, previously available only for wealthier, high-fee customers.

However, as you consider robo-advisors, it's important to assess their limitations. An algorithm might not be able to account for every nuance of your financial circumstances or market conditions.

9.4. Making Most of Your Budget

When it comes to budgeting, several tools can help you keep track of your spending and earnings. Mint, for example, allows you to set budgets for various categories and will alert you when you're coming close. You can track everything from weekly groceries to monthly bills, and even infrequent bills such as car insurance payments.

Automation can also be used to allocate funds to different accounts based on your budget. If you know your monthly groceries usually total $400, you can set that amount to be deducted from your paycheck directly into an account for groceries.

Never underestimate the power of a well-planned budget, and these tools make automating your budget easier than ever before.

9.5. Cashing in on the Power of Compound Interest

A key method of wealth accumulation is through compound interest. If you're not already taking advantage of this, automation can help. Set an automatic transfer that moves money from your checking account into a high-yield savings or investment account. The power of compound interest lies in investing over a long period of time.

Automating allows you to silently grow your wealth without the need for constant attention or management. Over time, you'll find your financial freedom increasing as your nest egg grows.

9.6. Optimizing Your Retirement Savings

Many people aim to be financially independent by the time they retire. One of the key steps towards achieving this is making the most of your retirement accounts. Tools like Blooom will analyze your 401(k) and show you if you're paying excessive fees or if you could change your investments to achieve greater returns.

Automation can help you continually deposit into your retirement accounts up to the appropriate limit. This can be particularly advantageous if your employer matches your contributions, as you'll be doubling your investment immediately.

Financial freedom isn't just about making money – it's about making your money work harder for you. By understanding and utilizing financial automation, we can all take a step toward greater financial independence. As the landscape continues to evolve, one thing remains constant: the quest for financial freedom is within your reach. Begin your journey today; after all, the future waits for nobody. Harness the potential of financial automation and let it pave the way for you to step into the era of wealth management.

Chapter 10. The Role of Artificial Intelligence in Financial Wellness

Artificial Intelligence (AI) has become an important player in the financial sector, bringing about a radical shift in the ways we manage our finances. While some might associate AI primarily with sophisticated tech ventures and small-to-mid-sized enterprises (SMEs), it's also making profound impacts in the personal finance landscape. Your smartphone, the personal finance app you use, the prompt customer service bot that assists you—each is laced with elements of AI, quietly helping manage your wealth more efficiently.

10.1. A Brief Introduction to AI

To appreciate the impact of AI on financial wellness, it's essential to understand what it is at its core. At the most basic level, AI is the capability of a machine or a software application to think and learn like a human— but with a key distinction. It can process vast amounts of information at light-speed, draw important insights, and make intelligent decisions free from emotional biases.

AI comes in various forms, including Machine Learning (ML), Natural Language Processing (NLP), and Deep Learning. Each has its unique way of remodeling personal finance, chasing efficiency, and boosting financial health.

10.2. How AI Contributes to Financial Wellness

AI is not just about efficiency; it's about effectiveness too. It makes personal finance management less cumbersome, yes, but it also makes it more strategic and less error-prone. Consider the following ways AI is securing your financial future:

1. **Automated financial advisers**: Known as robo-advisors, these AI-driven platforms provide automated, algorithm-based financial advice without human intervention. They analyze your financial goals, risk tolerance, and investment horizon to create personalized portfolios. As a result, you can make more informed financial decisions.

2. **Fraud detection and prevention**: AI algorithms can process thousands of transactions in a flash and quickly identify patterns that suggest fraudulent activities. They operate in real-time, alerting users to suspicious activity and keeping their financial health intact.

3. **Credit scoring**: Traditional credit scoring processes can be rigid and often miss out on the nuances of an individual's financial behavior. AI, with its capacity to analyze large and disparate data sets, can enable a more nuanced and accurate credit scoring system.

4. **Financial planning and budgeting**: AI-driven personal finance tools can analyze your spending habits, suggest smart saving tips, and even automate some elements of your financial planning. This not only streamlines your finance management but also prevents over-spending and under-saving.

10.3. Increasing Access to Financial Advice

One of the significant advantages of AI in personal finance is democratizing access to financial advice. Financial advice has traditionally been a privilege of the affluent because of the high costs associated with human financial advisors. Not anymore.

AI-driven platforms have significantly brought down these costs making financial advice accessible to all, irrespective of their wealth status. Tailored, data-driven advice, now readily available, opens a new horizon of financial wellness for all, including historically underserved demographics.

10.4. Safeguarding Privacy and Security

AI sits over a trove of sensitive financial data. While this might raise concerns about privacy and data security, AI developers and engineers continually refine the security protocols to prevent breaches. The use of encryption, multi-factor authentication, and advanced algorithms seek to ensure the data's integrity, making AI-driven tools as secure as traditional banking systems.

10.5. Empowering Financial Literacy

A financially literate population invariably forms the bedrock of a sound economy. AI can simplify financial concepts, translate complex financial language into comprehensible information, and encourage more and more people to participate in the financial system. In this way, AI can play a critical role in promoting financial literacy.

10.6. Promoting Financial Inclusion

By leveraging vast amounts of data and sophisticated algorithms, AI can facilitate access to financial services for those conventionally left outside the credit and banking system. This is particularly relevant for developing economies, where AI can play a significant role in driving financial inclusion.

Artificial Intelligence indeed is a game-changer in the world of personal finance and financial wellness. With AI at our fingertips, we can manage our personal finances like never before. We can make smarter decisions, plan better, save more, and secure our financial futures. As AI continues to evolve, we can only expect that its impact will be magnified – providing even more powerful tools for personal wealth management.

Chapter 11. The Potential Pitfalls of Automated Finance: A Balanced View

Even with the incredible benefits of automating personal finance, it is critical to view this innovation with a balanced perspective. Just like any technological advancement, automated finance has its set of potential pitfalls. This chapter provides you with an exhaustive overview of these risks, from the loss of personal touch to unexpected technical challenges and to the possible risks of over-reliance on technology.

11.1. Understanding the lack of Personal Touch

Historically, wealth management and personal finance have all been about relationships. You'd have your debt counselor, your financial advisor, or your banking relationship manager who knows you personally, comprehends your aspirations, and guides you throughout your financial journey. Technology, no matter how sophisticated, might not replace this level of personalized service yet.

An automation tool might not feel empathetic towards your volatile financial condition during a crisis. An algorithm will likely not understand if you're spending more due to a personal emergency. It doesn't share your joy when your budgeting efforts lead to surplus savings. This lack of personal touch and potential misunderstanding of financial nuances could lead to erroneous decisions, which can bring about catastrophic financial consequences.

11.2. Unexpected Technical Challenges

Even the best technology platforms are not entirely immune to periodic technical glitches and crashes. Just like how a storm can cause the internet or power to go down, software bugs or a hardware failure can affect your automated financial platform. Your vital financial data could be temporarily inaccessible or, in the worst case, suffer loss if plenty of redundancies are not in place. Furthermore, navigating these issues may require technical skills that not every user possesses, thus, potentially creating roadblocks.

11.3. Risk of Oversimplification

Weaving magic with automation relies on the ability to simplify complex tasks. But, the risk remains that this quest for convenience could lead to oversimplification. Financial planning is a meticulous task that requires considering a multitude of factors, including age, risk tolerance, current financial status, and long-term objectives. An automated tool might simplify this process to an extent that it becomes too generic, overlooking personal nuances, thus possibly leading to sub-optimal financial planning.

11.4. Possible Over-reliance on Technology

While leveraging current technological advances is wise, an over-reliance on it can set one up for financial mishaps. It can make one complacent, removing the necessity to understand the underlying principles of personal finance, economic trends, or market fluctuations. In such cases, when technology fails temporarily, or there are financial situations that the algorithm didn't factor, this lack of comprehension could leave one feeling helpless and panicked.

11.5. Data Security and Privacy Concerns

Automated personal finance platforms deal with highly sensitive financial data. Despite robust security measures being touted by providers, no platform is entirely immune to the threats of data breaches and malicious cyber-attacks. Such a scenario might expose users' personal data to the outer world, leading to severe financial loss and mental distress.

11.6. Risk of Limited Investments

Automated investment tools like robo-advisors can simplify the process of portfolio creation and management. However, these may limit users to pre-selected investments and asset classes. As a result, users may miss out on diversified alternative opportunities that could enhance their returns and diversify their portfolios further.

In conclusion, it's important to embrace the myriad opportunities that automated finance brings, yet at the same time, it's wise to be informed of its potential risks. Adopting a balanced view will help mitigate these risks and ensure that automated personal finance becomes a tool that truly amplifies your wealth management efficiency. As the saying goes, "Forewarned, forearmed; to be prepared is half the victory."